"Isolation, burnout, and depression are reality factors for people everywhere. They may be aggravated by the stresses of living overseas. This book should be a help to all who read it — especially mission leaders in the selection process and individual missionaries seeking help."
      Dr. David F. Brooks, Superintendent
      Morrison Academy, Taiwan

"Too many times people who aspire to be super missionaries, super pastors, et cetera, are unaware of what has happened to them as they begin to shrivel inside. They are unable to determine what has produced this result and certainly have little idea of what to do about it. In these pages Esther Schubert has given us the opportunity to look realistically at this situation and acknowledge that though we are wonderfully made, we have limitations. Healing and restoration are possibilities when we have passed those limits."
      David C. Pollock, Executive Director
      Interaction, Inc.

"Dr. Schubert has managed to 'speak down' from the high plateau of psychiatric jargon to address those of us who have to deal immediately with emotional distress in our mission groups. This book is down-to-earth, understandable, and usable — it meets a very real need."
      Dr. Rahn C. Strickler, Field Director
      OC International, Taiwan

"Missionaries, by the very nature of their task and environment, are placed at high risk for burnout and depression. Dr. Schubert clearly and concisely gives missionary leaders a valuable resource that will enable them to recognize these conditions and give wise direction to those who are suffering from them."
      Verona Dutton, Asst. Personnel Director
      SEND, International

What Missionaries Need to Know About Burnout and Depression

Esther Schubert, MD, FACEP, FAAFP

Olive Branch Publications
2239 N. Cadiz Pk., New Castle, IN 47362

Copyright © 1993 by Olive Branch Publications

Printed in the United States of America

To David

sine qua non

Contents

Foreword by Laura Mae Gardner ix
Preface xi
1. Missionaries and Burnout 1
2. Depression: Sources of Stress 9
3. Evidences of Bruising in Missionaries or Missionary Candidates 15
4. Depression as an Illness 21
5. Diagnosis of Major Depression 29
6. Adolescent Depression 33
7. Crisis Intervention for Depressed Adults and Adolescents 41
8. Childhood Depression (Pre-Adolescent) 45
9. Prevention of Burnout and Depression 49
Bibliography 59

Foreword

What is it that missionaries need to know about depression and burnout? I think they/we need to know three things: what it is; that it can happen to any one of us; what we can do about it for ourselves and others. I've needed to know those things because I've been depressed, not clinically so but enough to be hard to live with. And I've been close to burnout. The worst thing about these experiences is that I did not recognize what was happening. It takes an outside source, or an objective guideline to help us see what's going on in us. This book will assist us in these ways. The author of this book transparently shares her own experience of depression. You'll be comforted and encouraged when you read her personal experience. Some of you have had similar experiences. You'll appreciate what the author shares.

Missionaries live in some of the most stressful places on earth. It might be illegal to kill a mosquito — just blow it away; the temperature never gets below 90 day or night, there's no air conditioning and humidity is high. "I feel big, hairy, and sweaty most of the time." "I traveled down to Australia and put my son on the plane to return to the US; I sat in the hotel room waiting to return to our ministry location and reviewed my life as a father — and I grieved for all the things I did not do, and for this new stage in our lives, and for my wife alone back in our location." "The oppression and stress led to frustration, anger, irritability, and I actually hit him." "I could not eat or sleep for days."

If anyone knows these things with sympathy supported by personal experience, it is Esther Schubert. Lived in China, separated from her father during the revolution, all the moving, changes, stresses that go with cross-cultural living, war and disease and death, blended family, aloneness, marriage, childlessness, investment in needy children with no gratitude from them and little return — Dr. Schubert has experienced it all. She knows the mission field from the standpoint of amoebic dysentery and malaria, boarding schools, to experiencing it as a single woman, and then as a professional care-giver both on various fields, and by serving as a consultant and referral source when these dedicated people return to their home country and ask for her services.

She brings a nice blend of personal experience, professional training, medical expertise, psychiatric insight, and ability to tap the spiritual resources of Scripture. We should listen to her. I did. I hope you will.

> Dr. Laura Mae Gardner
> International Coordinator of
> Counseling Ministries and Personnel
> for Wycliffe & Summer Institute of
> Linguistics

September, 1992

Preface

Until recent years there has been a tendency in missionary circles to assume that Christians, and especially missionaries, should not be subject to burnout and depression. When suicide has occurred, the missionary community has been left with some awkward issues to address. If the traditional ideas are held rigidly, the community must regard these victims either as non-Christians, very weak Christians, or Christians with unresolved sin in their lives.

In recent years, however, we have seen a more balanced perspective. This approach holds that due to the fall of man we live in an imperfect world, and hence are vulnerable on three fronts — the spiritual, the physical, and also the mental or emotional. It is difficult for us as committed Christians to acknowledge our vulnerability in this third area. However, the record shows that individuals in Scripture, as well as fine Christians throughout the course of history have been afflicted with the mental illness known as depression. In this booklet we seek to address this topic in an effort to educate and inform missionaries, thus enabling them to seek and obtain proper treatment for depression should the need arise, and for burnout which may be a precursor to clinical depression.

The author wishes to express her appreciation for the patient work of Julia Shaffer in the preparation of this manuscript, and to Dr. Ed Erny for his invaluable and extensive editorial assistance.

CHAPTER 1

Missionaries & Burnout

I first became personally acquainted with burnout in the 1970s when I was working full-time, David and I were raising troubled adopted boys, tutoring these kids with their severe academic problems every night, and attempting to be a good wife, mother, and Christian. What had begun as a "honeymoon" of excitement and anticipation in working with these kids and helping to purchase a farm, quickly developed into fuel shortage where I continued to burn the candle at both ends but had run out of the necessary fuel. I began to develop chronic symptoms such as neck and back pain, severe headaches, and abdominal pain. I kept going by sheer discipline, committed to the project we were undertaking and by 1984 found myself in a profound depression.

In spite of my own assumed professional expertise, I had ignored the symptoms of burnout for eight years finally "hitting the wall," wishing I were dead, seeing no hope for the future, and requiring both antidepressants and psychotherapy to recover. With the help of friends, fellow professionals, and David, I did recover over the course of a year or so during which time I confronted my own childhood, primitive defense mechanisms, and a profound fear of separations and abandonment. I came to the conclusion that many of the things that I had perceived as altruistic, spiritual commitments in my life, were actually psychological agendas stemming from unfulfilled childhood needs and unhealthy adaptations to those needs. Burnout (and eventually depression) for me was a condition born of good intentions. I fell prey to it for consciously unselfish reasons, though I believe I was unconsciously driven to reach perfection in my career, as a wife, as a mother, and as a Christian. I pushed myself far too hard, far too long, and I failed to acknowledge my own limitations.

I have seen this pattern in missionary after missionary. I see it in missionary candidates and it often involves significant childhood issues and unconscious defense mechanisms which require lengthy psychotherapy. Untreated burnout may go on to depression because we feel a need to be disciplined and stoic and are therefore, insensitive to the warning signs of overload.

Burnout is usually a preliminary stage of depression. Recently, the term "burnout" has come into vogue in Western society to describe victims of excessive stress in the business world. It can also be applied to pastors, missionaries, and others in Christian ministry.

The words of an old gospel song say "Let me burn out for Thee, dear Lord." This worthy goal also finds expression in a frequently heard statement "Better burnout than rust out."

Dr. Wendell Friest, a psychologist and veteran missionary to Taiwan, points out that "If you think of burnout as something like what happens to an electric motor to prevent it from running too long at too high a speed, the choice of burning out rather than rusting out may well be a valid Christian attitude.... In psychological parlance, however, burnout means something different. The word is borrowed from rocketry science and refers to the point at which the fuel of a missile is completely expended. Using this conceptualization of the term, I don't think it is God's will that any of us 'burnout' during the days of our journey on earth.[1]"

How can one know that he or she is in danger of burnout and not simply experiencing normal reactions to hard work? Roy Oswald,[2] in his article on clergy burnout, identifies the following 16 symptoms

1. The tendency to feel negative or cynical about parishioners
2. Loss of enthusiasm for job
3. Lowered emotional investment in work
4. Fatigue and irritability
5. Cynical and sarcastic humor
6. Increased withdrawal from parishioners
7. Increased rigidity in dealing with parishioners
8. Feelings of isolation and lack of support
9. Frustration in accomplishing tasks
10. Increased feeling of sadness
11. Physical ailments
12. Lowered enjoyment of legitimate sexual activity with one's spouse
13. Tendency to blame others for problems
14. Tendency to feel guilty much of the time
15. Feeling of "just hanging on" until retirement
16. Sense of emptiness and depletion

Missionary life is stressful and almost always, by definition, strenuous and laborious. Burnout can occur at any time during missionary service but first-term missionaries may be the most vulnerable. Statistics suggest that about 15% of first-term missionaries bail out. Many of them have faced the exhaustion of fund-raising before going to the field. Culture shock often peaks at eight months into the first term. Language study may seem to be an unending, unsuccessful effort. The time frame of burnout is approximately two to three years into a new experience. Total immersion into a new culture, language and ministry creates all kinds of feelings that might never surface in any other situation.

Burnout can occur from two sources. The first is a system-generated burnout in which the situation may be untenable, organizational policies are not well-geared to the particular culture in which they have been incorporated, the bureaucracy is not in touch with the needs of individual missionaries, supervisory personnel are not suited for their jobs, the job does not permit time off or adequate rest, or there is no opportunity for let-down time (this often occurs, especially in live-in jobs such as dorm parenting, medical people on call 24 hours a day, etc.). In many mission settings the organization needs to take measures to modify the mission's expectations and to adjust to local and personnel needs.

A more difficult type of burnout often occurs due to the individual traits of the person involved. Perfectionists who live with "shoulds," "oughts," and the need to be in control may run on nervous energy and burn out quickly. Workaholics are often driven to live up to their own expectations or others' unrealistic expectations of them. Some of these individuals may have been the oldest child in their family and have developed a need for achieving control. Their workaholism can be a maladaptive method for controlling unexpected situations. Goal oriented missionaries are often frustrated in cultures in which time frames are less important than people skills. "Other oriented persons" need to be liked or admired. They are very sensitive to criticism and they may drive themselves to avoid it. They are generous to all but themselves and overidentify with and internalize the hurts of others. They may have the spiritual gifts of mercy and helps, see themselves as rescuers, and be motivated by social and interpersonal rewards. Other missionaries may lack assertive interpersonal skills, be unable to say "no," feel guilty when they express anger or other negative emotions, and have difficulty confronting. Finally, Minirth and Meier in their book *How to Beat Burnout*, devote an entire chapter to unresolved negative emotions such as bitterness as sources of burnout. Bitterness may occur due to unmet needs, personal loss, or sinful attitudes.

In general, system generated burnout tends to be clustered. One organization or one vocation or one field may have repeated performances of burnout in successive personnel. This is in contrast to burnout due to individual personality traits where there are more likely to be isolated cases of burnout since the source is more dispositional and personal. Of course, burnout can occur due to a combination of individual personality traits and untreatable external stresses or organizational malfunction.

Dr. Friest has reduced individual sources of burnout to two general personality types which he labels A-Type Syndrome and B-Type Syndrome.

A-Type personalities are those who are often described as "performance oriented Christians." For them, self-worth derives from accomplishments, from what they do. As long as they are able to perform acceptably they manage to survive; however, when as a result of fatigue, stress, or other factors, they cannot maintain the high standard of performance they demand of themselves, they begin to experience tremendous stress, falter, and begin burnout.

B-Type personalities are those who derive meaning and satisfaction from serving others. They give and give until there is literally no more to give. For them, that is when burnout becomes apparent.

Friest says that people in burnout sometimes feel like Garrison Keillor's Catholic church in rural Minnesota— Our Lady of Perpetual Responsibility. (How about that for a missionary wife's job description!) Under the right circumstances, this style—some people call it the "messiah complex" — produces a condition that he calls "compassion-fatigue."

Type-A missionaries display many of the characteristics of people prone to heart disease. Sehnert[3] lists ten of these characteristics:

1. Tendency to "overplan"
2. Multiple thoughts and actions
3. Need to win
4. Desire for recognition
5. Always feeling guilty
6. Impatient with delays or interruptions
7. Over-extended
8. Sense of time urgency
9. Excessive competitive drive
10. "Work-aholism"

Type-B missionaries, those who are addicted to helping, tend to manifest another set of characteristics. According to Tubesing[4], people addicted to helping give evidence of the following behavior traits:

1. A willingness always to give emotional support but seldom to ask or expect it from others
2. A feeling of selfishness when not responding to other people's needs
3. Excessive concern not to hurt other people's feelings
4. Determination to get a job done no matter what the cost to oneself
5. A desire to avoid conflict
6. A tendency to say "yes" too much and too often
7. A feeling that one "ought" to be able to help everyone
8. Sometimes, a sense of getting one's own needs met by helping others

What should you do if you recognize yourself as a Type-A or a Type-B syndrome individual whose behavior is all-too-well described in the above list?

Later on, when we deal with depression, we will discuss the strategy of stress management. I urge you to read this section carefully, pray about appropriate measures and ask God to help you incorporate them into your life.

Complete credits are published in the bibliography
[1]Friest, W. (Apr. 1992)
[2]Oswald, Roy (1982)
[3]Sehnert, Keith W. (1981)
[4]Tubesing, Nancy L. and Tubesing, Donald A. (1984)

CHAPTER 2

Depression: Sources of Stress

Ruth Bell Graham in her biography tells the story of a young missionary wife in China who committed suicide after months of profound depression[5]. This tragedy occurred in the 1930s in an era when depression was more often viewed as sin rather than sickness.

In 1984, two young adult missionary kids, graduates of the same overseas MK high school, committed suicide while living in the United States. These suicides opened the door for me to address the topic of "Suicide and Missionary Kids" at the Manila International Conference on Missionary Kids in the fall of 1984.

Depression seems to occur in individuals who have either a genetic predisposition toward this illness, severe chronic stress, or a combination of both the hereditary factors and stress.

Stress appears to be universal. There is no question that the life of a missionary and that of his/her children can be stressful. Today, many missionaries from the West have grown up with the conflicts inherent in a society marked by rootlessness, early exposure to drugs and alcohol, preoccupation with sex, and humanistic values. There do seem to be people, however, who never get depressed in their homeland yet encounter depression when they go overseas and face a different set of cultural values and stresses.

The first set of stresses revolves around the constellation of separations, rootlessness, and transitions. (See Table I.) The missionary kid often deals with separations at crucial life stages, particularly separations from parents, peers and other important people in his life. The adjustment of re-entry to the home country can also be stressful. Pollock says "unresolved grief is probably the primary issue in many MKs' lives."[6]

TABLE I

SOURCES OF MISSIONARY STRESS

1. Separations, rootlessness, transitions
2. Cultural stresses
3. Physical stresses & risks
4. Spiritual warfare
5. Interpersonal relationships
6. Administrative & organizational issues
7. Emotional bruising and old baggage

An adult missionary may also be affected by the separations of missionary life if separation was an issue in his or her childhood. This is especially the case if, as children, they had to deal with divorce, death, frequent moves (particularly if they, themselves, were missionary or military kids), or emotional bruising.[7] Missionaries often have to deal with separation from their home countries and families. Even adult missionaries reach the point where they are saturated with goodbyes and feel that they can only invest emotionally in a limited number of people.

A second stress that may cause depression in missionaries or missionary kids is that of cultural adjustment. For the MK and the retiring missionary, re-entry may actually create more cultural stress than living overseas. Vandenberg has described missionary kids at the time of re-entry as "invisible internationals."[8] Indeed, many missionary kids feel like strangers caught between two worlds. Their allegiances are many and none and they may have difficulty knowing where "home" is. The retiring missionary may have roots in his home country and yet have lived overseas so many years that he is accosted with a sense of homelessness upon retirement when he returns to his country of origin.

The adult missionary often suffers cultural stresses when he enters the foreign field. Language, food, sanitation, and the daily irritations of living in a culture where things are done differently, (where "yes" means "maybe" and where time-frames are modified), may create levels of stress unknown to those who have never lived cross-culturally.

A third area of difficulty occurs as a result of physical stresses and the risks of overseas living. There is a new awareness of the threat of missionaries acquiring AIDS. Also, parasites, malaria, and hepatitis continue to be ubiquitous overseas illnesses. Environmental hazards persist in some locations with an abundance of snakes, poisonous spiders, rats, and insects. Difficult climates in many parts of the world along with irritations such as bugs and mildew can be stressful, especially for foreigners deprived of many of their accustomed comforts and conveniences. As the majority of the world's population moves to urban areas, pollution, crowding, and noise intensify the problem. Added to this are political uncertainties, threats of war, and personal assaults which are part of life in many areas of the world.

The fourth problem is that of spiritual warfare which appears to be escalating in most parts of the world, including our own hemisphere. The addition of spiritual stressors to the others already mentioned may contribute to the pressures missionaries feel.

A fifth overseas stress often comes in the area of interpersonal relationships. This extends not only to interactions with the nationals, but the relationships between various members of the missionary team. Dorothy Gish[9] lists the inability to confront as the most frequent stressor encountered by missionary personnel. Pre-field psychological testing utilizing the MMPI*[10] suggests that a significant number of missionary applicants have a high need for affection which makes it difficult for them to confront colleagues, missionary or national. Many of these missionaries also utilize denial and repression as defense mechanisms and have limited capacity for insight as conflicts develop.

Administrative and organizational issues are a sixth arena in which stress and conflict may occur for the missionary. Submission to authority, mission structure, changes, matters of support, and constituency relationships all are vulnerable areas.

Finally, missionaries who get to the field with significant unresolved histories of emotional bruising may also be contending with a great deal of internal stress. This emotional baggage from the past can contribute to depression.[11] To uncover the factor of bruising it is

* Minnesota Multiphasic Personality Inventory

important that adequate testing be done prior to overseas missionary placement. Any of these stresses, if not dealt with effectively, can contribute to burnout or depression.

It is important to understand that by the term "depression" I am not referring to a low mood or a bad day but to a clinical illness, usually biochemically based, that occurs in Christians as well as in non-Christians. At any given time in North America five percent of the population is clinically depressed. One of eleven Americans will be hospitalized at some time in his or her life for depression. Depression seems to occur across all religious lines in almost the same way as appendicitis or strep throat, regardless of the person's Christian experience. The Scriptures reveal that conscientious, godly men such as Jeremiah contended with many of the symptoms of depression. Also, David appeared to meet many of the criteria of depression during the time that he was fleeing his enemies. Church history records that Charles Spurgeon, William Cowper, Martin Luther, and J. B. Phillips all had recurrent bouts of significant clinical depression.

Psychologists agree that there are predisposing factors to depression. The first is genetic susceptibility. We often find that individuals suffering from clinical depression have a significant number of blood relatives who are similarly afflicted.

Secondly, early traumatic experiences which can be traced to overly severe or dysfunctional families, losses, separations, or bruising all seem to predispose individuals to depression.

Finally, later psychological stress that echoes the early loss or rejection places unusual demands on the already vulnerable system, and may precipitate depression. The more trauma a person has experienced earlier in life, the more likely he is to develop psychological illness or depression after a stressful life event.

In many cases a missionary who was viewed as successful and well-adjusted in his own culture may find the move to a foreign culture the final straw in the precipitation of a depressive episode. This is particularly the case if issues of bruising, dysfunctional family background, and childhood trauma were not addressed prior to overseas placement.

[5]Cornwell, P. (pp. 23-24)
[6]Pollock, Dave, personal communication
[7]Powell, J. (1987)
[8]Vandenberg, T. (1985)
[9]Gish, D. (1983)
[10]Schubert, E. (1992)
[11]O'Donnell, K. & Schubert, E. (1992)

CHAPTER 3

Evidences of Bruising in Missionaries or Missionary Candidates

In many cases adults who have experienced emotional bruising in their childhood do not realize how this affects their adult adjustments. As mentioned previously, these vulnerabilities can be detected with good psychological testing, particularly the use of the MMPI in pre-field evaluations.[12]

In addition, individuals may be aware of problem areas in their lives, especially tensions between things as they are and things as they ought to be—known in psychological terms as "discrepancies."[13] (See Table II.) I see four kinds of discrepancies in missionaries and missionary candidates.

TABLE II

FOUR DISCREPANCIES (Schubert, 1989)

1. Emotional discrepancy
2. Physical discrepancy
3. Discrepancy in intensity
4. Discrepancy between facts and feelings

First, emotional discrepancies (or emotions with unknown causes such as crying and angry outbursts for no apparent reason) may indicate that there are unconscious areas which profoundly affect current behavior. (It is important to rule out other causes such as hormonal changes or organic factors that may play a part).

Secondly, physical discrepancies such as psychosomatic illnesses often indicate unresolved emotional issues. Such physical illnesses have no biological basis and do not respond to the usual treatments. Marjorie Foyle, at the International Conference on Missionary Kids in Quito in 1987, suggested that there are at least five psychosomatic disorders indicating masked depression in adult missionaries. They are: 1) Pain in the face, especially common in women. This pain tends to be worse in the morning and is often accompanied by early morning awakening. 2) Chronic colon symptoms for which medical reasons cannot be found. 3) Impotence in men—if no physical explanation can be elicited. These men may also awaken early in the morning for no apparent reason. 4) Headaches that seem to be more intense in the morning. 5) Weakness which also may be more apparent in the morning.

All five of these problems are without organic cause and tend to be worse in the morning. The following is an example.

CASE STUDY #1 (Depression with somatization)

Phyllis Schmidt* was a 30-year-old single missionary in Africa. She began to develop physical problems during her second year of missionary service. She first complained of headaches,

* Names in all case studies have been changed.

severe in the morning and tending to diminish later in the day. She had a chronic problem with colitis, which was determined not to be due to parasites or other medical problems. Phyllis soon found that she was extremely tired almost all of the time. In spite of her fatigue, she awakened early each morning. In time, she became very disillusioned with the medical help available since doctors were unable to find physical causes for her problems.

She was seen by a therapist who did a clinical interview and administered the MMPI.** The therapist believed that Phyllis was clinically depressed and that this depression was manifesting itself in physical symptoms. At first, Phyllis had difficulty acknowledging the emotional causes of her illness.

After several sessions with the therapist and consulting with medical doctors, however, she eventually agreed to a trial of antidepressants combined with continuing counseling.

After 18 months of therapy Phyllis was beginning to acknowledge some emotional sources for her physical symptoms and she showed improvement. Her insight continued to be limited, however, and it was easy for her to fall back into defense mechanisms such as denial and repression. Happily, she was able to continue her missionary work, agreeing that during her next furlough she would be scheduled for more in-depth therapy.

** Minnesota Multiphasic Personality Inventory

A third discrepancy is a discrepancy in intensity. By this I mean emotional reactions out of proportion to the event. In many cases, the exaggerated response is triggered by a seemingly insignificant event, but one which symbolizes earlier traumatic losses.

Fourth is a discrepancy between facts and feelings. This occurs when an individual feels something strongly and yet the facts do not warrant that interpretation. Often there are times when the person involved is not aware of the discrepancy but others looking on can clearly see that there is a significant gap between the facts of the events and the person's perception of them.

Any of these four discrepancies may indicate unconscious, unresolved psychological issues.

CASE STUDY #2 (Depression with bruising, genetic factors and external stress)

> John A. Nelson, a 35-year-old missionary to South America comes from a dysfunctional family. His parents were divorced when he was ten years of age and he had suffered significant abuse. His paternal grandmother and his mother both had histories of depression. Also, a distant relative was thought to have been a manic depressive.
>
> John became a Christian in his early 20s and testified to feelings of great peace, security and love. He expressed the hope that he would be able to serve the Lord at some time in the future. Eventually, he felt inclined toward missionary service. He entered Bible school and began preparation toward that end.
>
> John completed his training, applied to a mission board, and was accepted for service in Ecuador.

John found the transition to another culture to be very difficult and did not do well in language study. Eventually, he and his wife began to have marital difficulties and one of his two children also displayed adjustment problems. Soon John was experiencing sleeping difficulties, a decrease in appetite including weight loss, problems concentrating, and low self esteem. At times he struggled with a preoccupation with death and seemed to have an inordinate amount of guilt. He began to misinterpret people's motivations where the facts were obviously contrary, he often cried on minor provocation, and he had some angry outbursts that seemed entirely out of character for him.

When it became apparent that John's problems were not limited to culture shock, he was referred to a missionary psychiatrist in a neighboring country. This professional diagnosed John as having a major depressive episode for which he was administered antidepressants. In addition, the doctor believed that John had some unresolved childhood issues including bruising, which would require long-term counseling. Due to the unavailability of nearby professional help, the mission decided to send John and the family back to the United States for therapy, family and marital counseling, and ongoing medication management.

[12]O'Donnell, K. & Schubert, E. (1992 in press)
[13]Schubert, E. (1989)

CHAPTER 4

Depression As An Illness

In this book I am discussing depression as an illness and not as a sin. It is important, however, to remember that sin in a person's life can and will produce emotional havoc. There are consequences to behavior and we do reap what we sow. In my experience as a clinician, however, most of the depression I see in missionaries stems from illness rather than unconfessed sin. In these cases I find that spiritual matters have been dealt with long before I am consulted. If spiritual issues are at the core, and when dealt with will solve the problem, missionaries usually do not come to see me. Unfortunately, I do occasionally see depressed missionaries who have had a great deal of false guilt placed on them by well-meaning fellow Christians who have implied that their underlying problem is, indeed, sin. This adds to the burden of suffering. For that reason, what I am referring to here is clinical depression which, by definition, is a biochemical illness which often makes the pain of living more terrible than that of dying. In such cases depressed persons, even Christians, may look at suicide as a way out. Many Christians have told me that in the depth of their depression, they have felt that there was no possible physical pain to compare with the emotional pain they were suffering.

Crisis intervention, then, addresses three issues. First, the immediate prevention of suicide, if it is a danger/threat. Second, gradual relief of severe emotional pain. And third, prevention or amelioration of further depressive episodes.

A significant article entitled "Baby Boomer Blues" appeared in the journal *Psychology Today* in October, 1988. The author's contention is that we are increasingly vulnerable to depression in Western society because we now have a new generation with increased expectations, a sense of entitlement (the feeling that the world owes them a living), and decreased institutional loyalty. These people have come to expect immediate gratification—a T.V. mentality that says "Here is the product and you can have it now!" This generation is markedly materialistic, has had access to drugs and sex at an early age, and is producing very unstable families. Too sophisticated to value patriotism, they also have difficulty submitting to authority. This baby boomer generation is the pool from which we are recruiting many of our current missionaries. This suggests to me that we can expect to see an increased incidence of depression in missionary candidates who are baby-boomers and the children of baby-boomers.

I will discuss depression using some older terminology and then correlate it with current usage. In older literature, depression tended to be categorized as either endogenous or exogenous (see diagram). Endogenous depression usually means a depression that has a biochemical base and is considered to be a physical illness. By contrast, exogenous depression is a reaction to real or

Depression Diagram

Bipolar Biochemical Depression (Suicidal Risk)

Unipolar Biochemical Endogenous Depression (Suicidal Risk)

Exogenous Depression

CURRENT TERMINOLOGY:

MAJOR DEPRESSION

UNCOMPLICATED BEREAVEMENT
or
ADJUSTMENT DISORDER

COMPLICATED BEREAVEMENT
or
COMPLICATED ADJUSTMENT DISORDER

MAJOR DEPRESSION (BIPOLAR)	MAJOR DEPRESSION (UNIPOLAR)	BEREAVEMENT OR ADJUSTMENT DISORDER
Sources: 　Biochemical	Sources: 　1. Prolonged stress 　　　a. External 　　　b. Internal 　2. Pathologic grief, anger, guilt, or fear 　3. Idiopathic 　4. Hormones 　5. Medications	Sources: 　1. Losses 　2. Transitions
Treatment: 　Lithium 　Tegretol 　Valproate	Treatment: 　1. Medications — 　　　TCA, Prozac or MAO 　2. ECT 　3. Counseling (clinical)	Treatment: 　1. Tincture of time 　2. Support systems 　3. Counseling 　　　(clinical or pastoral)

perceived loss of a loved one, place, possession, pride, self esteem, job, or status. Grief is an example of exogenous depression, as is culture shock. Usually, exogenous depression is caused by acute, external stress. It is usually self-limited and sufferers are not likely to commit suicide. If grief after the loss of a spouse or other traumatic experience persists unabated for more than a year, there may be a pathological process at work rather than uncomplicated bereavement.[14] In the diagram this is symbolized by the area of overlapping circles.

Endogenous depression, often termed "major depression," is more likely to be a central nervous system dysfunction. Chemicals in the body and brain have been depleted resulting in serious emotional disturbance.

There are medical illnesses such as malaria, hepatitis, anemia, mononucleosis, and others that can give a strong feeling of depressed mood. These should be ruled out before a person is diagnosed as having major or endogenous depression. After medical causes have been excluded, there seem to be various underlying precipitants for major or endogenous depression. First is prolonged stress, either internal or external. This includes untreated burnout. Second, unresolved negative emotions such as pathologic grief, anger, or guilt. Third, what is termed idiopathic biochemical depression. This occurs when there is a chemical depletion even though the individual may have experienced no great trauma or bruising. This so called "no fault depression" is strongly influenced by heredity. Fourth, (there is some debate about this), evidence suggests that hormonal changes can cause a type of biochemical depression. This can occur in cycles with certain types of pre-menstrual syndrome. The hormonal stresses of menopause may also trigger an underlying endogenous depression. Fifth, there are some medications such as Reserpine (formerly used for high blood pressure) which can deplete the neuro-transmitters and cause depression.

The treatment for endogenous depression (with the exception of bipolar or manic-depressive type) is first, to replenish the depleted chemicals using medications. Individuals who do not respond to antidepressants may need ECT—electro-convulsive therapy. In the right hands this can be done very effectively and is a good second line treatment when medications have not worked. Third, with both of the above treatments counseling is also necessary, especially if there are underlying emotional causes of chemical depletion.

There is one other kind of chemical depression called bipolar depression. This was formerly referred to as manic-depressive illness due to the fact that the sufferers often alternate between states of hyperactivity and immobilizing depression. The treatment for this illness differs slightly from that used for unipolar depression. Medications are usually lithium, Tegretol or valproic acid which are used as mood stabilizers. *It is critically important for these medications to be prescribed and monitored by an experienced physician.* At times of depression, antidepressants may be added to the mood stabilizer. For bipolar patients antidepressants are not used by themselves as they may precipitate a manic episode.

Statistics tell us that if victims of unipolar or bipolar depression are not treated, there is a 15-25 percent chance that they will eventually commit suicide. Depression can be a terminal illness.

CASE STUDY #3 (Uncomplicated bereavement, exogenous depression)

James Keller is a 56-year-old missionary to Malaysia. A widower, his wife had died suddenly of cerebral malaria while on the field. James had a strong network of friends and colleagues and initially appeared to weather this crisis well. In fact, it was noticed that he showed few of the normal signs of grief during the early period of bereavement. Nevertheless, after several months he began to have difficulty sleeping, easily gave way to tears, lost weight, and always looked sad.

James was seen by a therapist in the nearby capitol city who diagnosed his problem as an "uncomplicated bereavement episode." The counselor arranged to see him on a regular basis for supportive therapy over a period of six months. As a result, James was able to continue to work effectively at his profession. No medication was required.

Two years after his wife's death, James fell in love with a single missionary and they were eventually married. Today, he continues to keep an active and productive schedule and seems to have made a complete recovery.

As illustrated by the case of James Keller, those who suffer from exogenous depression seldom require medication. This type of depression is sometimes called bereavement or adjustment reaction. For most of these people, passage of time, support systems, and counseling are adequate treatment.

Occasionally, an individual may have a simple bereavement or adjustment reaction which later develops into a full-fledged depressive episode. In this case, the normal grief probably triggered or uncovered an underlying major depression.

At this point, one additional type of depression needs to be mentioned. People with deep-seated personality disorders may seek therapy for a type of depression which is far less treatable than those previously mentioned. Many of these clients come for help because their problem has created so much discomfort that they feel depressed. Unfortunately, the personality disorder needs to be treated before the depression will begin to lift. The treatment of personality disorder often takes years and is best accomplished in one's own country. The limited mental health care available in mission settings is not usually adequate for long term psychiatric therapy.[15]

---

[14]Nuss, W. (1992)
[15]Schubert, E. (1991, 1992, 1993)

CHAPTER 5

Diagnosis of Major Depression

It is important for mission leaders and other missionaries to recognize symptoms of major depression. In many isolated areas of the world field leaders or administrators have to deal with extremely serious personnel problems and it is helpful if they can utilize scientific criteria in making a tentative diagnosis and referring the patient for help. On many mission fields, adequate treatment is simply not available and tentative diagnosis will help in making decisions as to whether the depressed individual needs to be relocated to obtain medical or psychiatric care.

The DSMIIIR* criteria for major depression are as follows:

A. At least five of the following symptoms appear within a two week period and at least one of the symptoms must be either a depressed mood or a loss of interest or pleasure.

*American Psychiatric Association, Diagnostic and Statistical Manual, 3rd Edition, revised.

1. Depressed mood
2. Markedly diminished interest or pleasure in all or almost all activities
3. Significant weight loss/gain, decrease/increase in appetite
4. Insomnia or oversleeping nearly every day
5. Overactivity or underactivity
6. Fatigue or loss of energy
7. Feelings of worthlessness or inappropriate guilt
8. Decreased concentration or inability to think clearly
9. Recurrent thoughts of death, recurrent suicidal thoughts and/or plans

B. 1. The symptoms are not due primarily to an organic or medical illness
2. Symptoms are not merely a reaction due to the death of a loved one (uncomplicated bereavement)

C. Delusions or hallucinations accompanying severe depression must not have been present when patient was not depressed

D. There is no other psychiatric illness

It is important to distinguish a major depressive episode from other kinds of low-mood because of the immediate need for medications, suicide precautions, and eventually clinical counseling.

A word needs to be said about the use of Scripture with the acutely depressed. As missionaries, we base our lives upon Scripture, its admonitions and its promises. In the depths of a major depressive episode, however, an individual may be unable to assimilate the benefits of

Scripture. More than this, due to distorted perceptions and feelings of failure, Scripture may actually add to feelings of guilt. As Tournier observes, depressed patients often gravitate to the "wrong" Scripture passages, ones that speak of judgment and condemnation, confirming their own feelings of guilt and worthlessness. As I mentioned previously, in most cases, by the time people seek professional psychological care for their depression, they have already tried spiritual remedies and may have come to the conclusion that the problem is not spiritual. In addition, if friends or colleagues have simply quoted them Scripture verses in an effort to find a quick cure, the depressed individual may begin to resent the fact that others do not understand the depth of his or her psychological pain. For this reason, I don't use a great deal of counseling or Scripture in the early treatment of major depression. The analogy I would draw is that of an individual who is vomiting from viral gastroenteritis and is not able to physically assimilate a steak. The steak is, in fact, excellent nourishment but the person is simply not able to utilize the benefits of a steak at that time. Thus, in the throes of profound depression, one usually cannot assimilate the benefits of Scripture. He may, in fact, see it as a superficial answer which does not address the extreme pain that he is feeling. Later on in the counseling sessions, after antidepressants have taken effect, use of Scripture and other types of counseling are more appropriate.

CHAPTER 6

Adolescent Depression

Until about 15 years ago, many psychiatric professionals thought that depression occurred only in adults. We now realize that it frequently occurs in teenagers and in even younger children. We have actually seen a five-fold increase in psychiatric illness in older teenagers during the past 40 years. We are realizing as we counsel adult depressives that many of them, in retrospect, showed the first signs of depression as teenagers or even when they were children. Some young adults with depression have told me that they remember being depressed as early as five or six years of age. Unfortunately, the earlier the onset, the more severe the disease and the more likely it is to recur. The vulnerable adolescent often is the one who suffered losses at critical childhood ages. The symptoms of depression in adolescents are similar to those in adults, although somewhat different from those of younger children. In adolescents we see the following:

1. Disturbed mood, sadness, boredom, pessimism
2. Low self esteem

3. Poor concentration or decreased school performance
4. Sleep changes
5. Appetite changes or weight changes
6. Physical complaints
7. Suicidal preoccupation
8. Withdrawal, which may often be interpreted as resolution (improvement)
9. Acting out or running away

It is characteristic that adolescents often do not perceive that their unusual behavior relates to their feelings. Depressed adolescents, as well as adults, may have a family history of depression and may also be dealing with some environmental stresses. Many come from dysfunctional families or have parents who come from this type of home and as a result have poor parenting skills.

In the U.S. in the past 20 years there has been a severe erosion of sources of self esteem. There have been losses of religious identity, family cohesiveness, and patriotism. In MKs stress may be compounded by constant moving resulting in a sense of rootlessness and the loss of the extended family.

Adolescence is a chaotic time of life marked by various stages of development. At age 12, the child is still often dependent on his parents but by 13 or 14, his peers are everything to him. He craves identity within his peer group and feels he must have a group of friends to survive. By age 15 or 16 he may be thinking more in terms of a single heterosexual friend and by age 17 we hope he is beginning to establish his own identity and to develop a mature super ego or conscience.

Due to the importance of peers in the 13-15 year age group, I believe that this period in a child's life may be the most dangerous time to make a move, either to the mission field or a return to live permanently in the homeland. This trauma may be exacerbated even more for an only child. (I do not consider furlough moves as permanent moves.)

Adolescents pass through these stages of development differently. Occasional adolescents make a smooth, gradual transition in the direction of maturity. For others, it is an irregular uncertain process with periodic crises interspersed with times of relative calm. Other adolescents seem to spend all their teenage years in tumult. This time of life is difficult because teenagers are attempting to achieve three goals. (See Table III.) First, separation and individuation; second, the establishment of a lifetime identity; and third, the development of a mature super ego or conscience. During this time the teenager needs the security of a stable home yet he also needs to break away. He may act like an adult one day and more like a two-year-old the next.

TABLE III

DEVELOPMENTAL TASKS OF ADOLESCENCE

1. Separation and individuation
2. Establishment of lifetime identity
3. Development of a mature super ego and conscience

Teenagers, including MKs, deal with stress in a variety of ways (Table IV). Some rebel and to a degree, this is normal and cause for no special concern unless the child becomes excessively destructive, delinquent, or begins to withdraw. Others may resort to fantasy. This is not a serious problem unless it goes beyond normal daydreaming into drugs, alcohol, the occult, mind games such as Dungeons and Dragons, or acid rock music. There is particular cause for concern if these activities occupy large blocks of his or her time. Finally, some adolescents react to stress by becoming depressed.

TABLE IV

METHODS OF COPING WITH ADOLESCENCE

1. Rebellion
2. Fantasy
3. Depression

Ross Campbell, M.D.[16] comments that "the thing that makes adolescent depression so dangerous is that it may be hard to detect, it develops slowly, and it may be masked." In many teenagers depression expresses itself in masked symptoms called "depressive equivalents." They may have physical symptoms, develop an eating disorder, or appear happy when they really are sad. "Smiling depression" may be detected in the teen who appears happy when he is with his friends but looks sad when he feels no one is watching. In some cases, adults know when they are depressed whereas a teenager, more often, does not know.

Dr. Campbell lists the symptoms of light teenage depression as follows:

1. Lack of concentration
2. Daydreaming
3. Shorter attention span

4. Calling oneself names
5. Lowered grades

Moderate depression may be evidenced by:

1. A deep-rooted boredom in which the teenager may engage in activities to distract from boredom. Boys often act out with antisocial behavior, seeking dangerous excitement to escape boredom, or they may get involved in drugs, alcohol, mind games and violence. Girls more often act out with sexual promiscuity, shoplifting, and eating disorders. It should be noted that recent studies have shown that low serotonin levels (one of the neuro-transmitters) in boys are associated with acting out aggressively whereas many girls direct their hostility inward. In either case, low serotonin levels may be associated with poor impulse control.
2. Disinterest in surroundings
3. Withdrawal
4. Physical symptoms
5. Eating changes
6. Lack of energy

Dr. Campbell states that the following symptoms appear if the teenager progresses to a state of severe depression:[17]

1. Thought processes are affected
2. Loss of ability to think clearly, logically, and rationally
3. Deteriorating judgment
4. Focusing on morbid details
5. Assuming all is bleak, nothing is worthwhile, and life is not worth living

If severe depression goes on long enough there may be permanent biochemical damage. Although depression tends to be cyclical (that is, it comes and goes), it is dangerous to assume that it will resolve itself.

By the time a teenager has thought distortion he loses the ability to think and communicate in a clear and rational way and counseling becomes less and less effective. He may become self destructive or he may run away.

Of course, severe depression can lead to suicide. It often falls to the adults to make decisions regarding suicide intervention for a depressed teenager.

Boys succeed at suicide three times more often than girls. They also tend to use more violent, final, and lethal methods such as guns, hanging, and jumping. There is usually less chance of intervention with these methods. In recent years, however, women have become more assertive and we see more girls, as well as adult women, resorting to violent methods.

It is important to remember that chronic stress, even in teenagers, can bring on depression. Compliant children are particularly prone to depression as well as to eating disorders. Very sensitive, they may be depressed just because there are problems in the world. The reverse is also true. Some depressed youth try to cope with their low moods by becoming very compliant. A child like this may be genetically vulnerable to stress and becomes compliant in an effort to avoid confrontation. Often, he or she seems fine until the teen years when sent to boarding school and separated from home. At this point, without the support of his family, he may be unable to cope. This can then precipitate depression or suicide.

Above all we must not assume that adolescent depression is a phase. It is, rather, an **illness which requires intervention** before it results in death or permanent disability.

Experiments have shown that even monkeys can be depressed. One study found that young monkeys with a high genetic tendency toward depression, if placed in a colony with extremely nurturing mothers, respond well. This seems to indicate that the genetic susceptibility can be overcome with environmental modification. I am convinced that the susceptible, vulnerable child, if discovered early enough, can be helped. In boarding school the MK who fits the category of the vulnerable child by nature or lack of nurture should, if possible, be placed with particularly nurturing dorm parents or teachers.

According to Bill Blackburn Christian teenagers commit suicide for all the usual reasons plus a few additional ones.

These include:

1. They feel that they are trapped in an intolerable situation (this can be either real or perceived). Though their perception may be inaccurate it must be remembered that the threat is real.
2. They desire to join a loved one in heaven.
3. They have an overly romantic view of death.
4. They have a distorted Christian view, seeing heaven as an escape.
5. They feel they have committed the unpardonable sin.
6. They are victims of immaturity or impulsiveness.
7. They have some form of mental illness.

One danger many MKs face is that they seem to be very achievement oriented.[18] MKs are frequently burdened with high expectations—their own and others'. At some point, missionaries as well as MKs must learn that no amount of achievement can compensate for loss of early love and unconditional acceptance.[19]

Occupational success is not simply one goal in Western culture, it is the outstanding trait. Thus, to get ahead and succeed we feel we must hold ourselves to extremely high standards of personal excellence. Unfortunately, we have carried this outlook with us into the third culture. Somehow we must learn to communicate that our self esteem, either as missionaries or as MKs, is based on our relationship with Christ and not on our performance athletically, academically, or even spiritually.

[16]Kessler, J., Campbell R., (1984, p. 201)
[17]Kessler, J., Campbell R., (1984, p. 202)
[18]Danielson, E. (1982)
[19]Maris, R. (1981, p. 129)

CHAPTER 7

Crisis Intervention for Depressed Adults and Adolescents

In the area of crisis intervention what can be done on the mission field for the depressed adult or adolescent?

First, it is important to understand the different types of depression and the available treatments (Table V).

TABLE V

CRISIS INTERVENTION

1. Understand different types of depression
2. Know how to detect and diagnose depression
3. Investigate suicide potential
4. Disposition decisions/arrangements for treatment

Second, as missionaries we must learn to recognize depression and know the symptoms that are clear indicators of this illness.

Third, we must know how to evaluate the possibility or likelihood of suicide. When a missionary or teenage MK appears to be depressed and evidences symptoms of a major depressive episode, it is important that a qualified person talk with him/her to determine the suicidal potential. It is cause for alarm if the person is feeling hopeless and also if he/she is giving things away, talking as if there is no future, wrapping up affairs, or appearing to give up. Also, the investigator should ask directly if the individual has considered suicide.

For many years there was a myth that asking a person about suicide potential might put the idea into his or her mind. The fact is that if a person is depressed enough, thoughts of suicide have occurred to him and it may be a great relief to be honest and to talk about the "unmentionable." If the individual has thought about suicide, it helps to know if he has a plan and how well thought out it is. If there is a plan, what has kept him from carrying it out? How lethal is the method? How lethal does he think the method is? Forethought and planning are ominous indicators of a serious threat of suicide.

Fourth, personnel on the field need to decide if care is available in that location or if the individual needs to be taken, under supervision, to another location. If a person can make a verbal or written commitment to avoid suicide and to cooperate with out-patient therapy (assuming it is available), it may be possible for him or her to avoid hospitalization. On the other hand, a depressed missionary or MK who will not agree to measures to prevent self-destruction must be under some type of 24-hour-a-day supervision.

The treatment for endogenous depression begins with appropriate medication. Tricyclic antidepressants, Prozac, or MAO inhibitors are the most common medications in use. These are non-addictive and can be given to either adolescents or adults. Administration of antidepressants needs to be combined with counseling and the medications must be carefully monitored by a physician trained in their use. It is usually important for the client to stay on antidepressants for at least a full year. One should also know that it usually takes three to four weeks for the medication to take effect. At times, when the patient first starts to improve, he is at greater risk of suicide due to the fact that increased energy level may enable him to act on suicidal wishes. He is no longer paralyzed by misery, although he is still sick enough to want to die. Unfortunately, tricyclic antidepressants have a significant overdose potential and administration of these drugs must be carefully controlled and monitored.

Again, I emphasize that these medications are not generally the sole treatment for unipolar depression but are used in conjunction with psychotherapy (counseling). The therapist should be a professional, trained and experienced in psychotherapeutic practice. Pastoral counseling is usually not adequate in these cases. (Antidepressants should not be used alone in bipolar patients.)

CHAPTER 8

Childhood Depression (Pre-Adolescence)

Childhood depression can be very difficult to treat and may indicate pathology in the family structure. Chronic childhood depression occurs in about 2% of pre-adolescent (aged 7-12) children in the United States. These children are often dry-eyed (rather than tearful) and I seldom attempt to treat them in the overseas setting. In many cases, the entire family needs therapy and the mission field may not be the best place to find adequate professional counseling.

Occasionally, children may become acutely distressed and fearful but only for a brief period of time. This situation is primarily milder exogenous depression and can be treated on the field. However, the following signs are indications of a more chronic (endogenous) and serious type of childhood depression not usually treatable overseas:

1. Appears sad or unhappy
2. Withdrawn socially or hyperactive (In such cases it is important to first rule out the possibility of

attention deficit/hyperactivity disorder)
3. Experiences feelings of being unwanted or unloved and may, if asked, express these feelings
4. Perceives self in a negative light
5. Difficulty in controlling aggressive drives—fighting, biting, destructive behavior and aggression toward people or things
6. Excessive bullying or teasing
7. Public defecation
8. Enuresis (bedwetting)
9. Insomnia, although not particularly early morning awakening such as is characteristic of adult depressives
10. Excessive auto-eroticism (the key word here is excessive; many children indulge in occasional masturbation which is not generally considered to be pathologic)
11. Psychosomatic symptoms
12. Presence of hereditary factors (often one of the parents is depressed)
13. Victim of abuse—physical, emotional, verbal or sexual
14. Obvious separation anxiety, even to the extent of "school phobia"
15. Development of eating disorders, especially in older children

In chronic childhood depression the child often has difficulty relating to others—parents, teachers, friends—and may be clinging or cynical. In such cases there is frequently a family history of endogenous depression and the entire family may also be in need of counseling.

Age is a critical factor in childhood suicide. Between birth and five years children consider death to be reversible ("He will wake up"). This may be immaturity or the result of viewing cartoons in which characters fall off a cliff and get up and walk away. Between the ages of five and nine children consider death to have both good and bad attributes. Between nine and twelve the child develops a more mature concept of death. Because few suicides occur during this period we consider this the "suicide latency age." Age twelve to fourteen is a gray area in terms of suicide frequency.

CHAPTER 9

Prevention of Burnout & Depression

I believe that often depression can be prevented by early intervention and wise conservation of personal resources. In some situations, missionaries become burned out before they progress into depression (see illustration). As we noted earlier, burnout for some people may be thought of as an early stage of depression and is often evidenced by a tendency to continue to take on more than one can handle. Often these individuals keep going by sheer self-discipline. They may develop chronic physical symptoms and eventually get to a point where they can no longer continue at the same relentless pace. Others progress to depression without the intermediate phase of burnout.

HEALTHY — — → BURNOUT — — → DEPRESSION

Burnout is a special danger to the missionary who finds himself in a totally new situation, faced with a completely unanticipated event over which he has little or no control. Added stress occurs when he has no responsive social support systems.

Burnout and some cases of depression may be prevented by the following:

1. Learning to "off load" emotionally. This requires being in touch with one's own feelings, keeping short accounts (not allowing grudges and frustrations to build up in personal relationships), and dealing with issues as they occur.
2. Learning to say "no" when one is asked to do more than is reasonable.
3. Being alert to desperate feelings and understanding the emotional implications of those feelings. It may help to consider a worst-case scenario in an effort to defuse the subliminal unconscious fears. This helps the individual confront the "what if" and to acknowledge the adequacy of God's grace.
4. Eating a regular and balanced diet.
5. Making time for meaningful relationships and fellowship, keeping the capacity for laughter. Remember "A merry heart doeth good like a medicine."
6. Exercise. Missionaries need to schedule time to exercise on a regular basis understanding that exercise releases body chemicals called endorphins which lift the mood and help in depression prevention.
7. Devotional life. Our devotional life compensates for the fact that many spiritual goals are nebulous. It provides us with the encourage-

ment and sense of God's presence in the good times as well as the difficult ones.

8. Paying attention to sleep needs and remembering that God is more interested in us than in our work. David A. Seamands once commented that we are not "God's cosmic pets." If we abuse our bodies and minds, they will eventually wear out.

9. Maintaining a commitment to the "law of the Sabbath." All of creation is geared to one day of rest per week. God set the example at creation and Jesus continued that in Mark 6:31 when He said "Let us get away from the crowds and rest." The consequences of not observing the Sabbath are catastrophic whether for the individual, the mission, the nation, or a profession.

Factories in the United States which have tried to go on seven-day-work weeks to increase production have experienced an increased incidence of absenteeism and illness.

There are also at least two historical examples from the Old Testament suggesting the critical need for rest. The first example is when the Israelites were in Egypt for 400 years. They were not viewed as human beings but as producers of bricks—slaves. When we as missionaries begin to see others in terms of what they can do, not who they are, we deface humanity and damage the missionary community. God's order is grace first (relationship) and work second (even His). When we reverse God's order we get into trouble.

The second example of the law of the Sabbath is when Judah was in captivity in Babylon for 70 years. This came as a consequence of omitting the Sabbath rest for 490 years. It is most noteworthy that in II Chronicles 36:21 the Scripture comments that the nation would be in captivity until the days of its Sabbaths had been completed. Seventy years, of course, is exactly 1/7th of 490 years.

In conclusion, I would like to quote from the excellent article entitled "The Understanding and Prevention of Missionary Burnout" by Dr. Wendell Friest, the previously quoted missionary in Taiwan. He says:

To prevent burnout, the beginning point for missionaries is our conception of who we are in relation to God and to the world. The most helpful formulation of this that I have found is Martin Luther's definition of the freedom of a Christian: "A Christian is a perfectly free lord of all, subject to none. A Christian is a perfectly dutiful servant of all, subject to all."

To really believe this—and to live accordingly—seems to me to involve a two-stage process of spiritual development. The first stage is to move from a slave-modality kind of Christianity into a daughter-son modality. The second stage is to return to a slave modality without ever losing the daughter-son modality. Our example for this is Jesus himself, who is both the Son of God and the suffering servant—the joyful slave of God. Consider these two ways in which he described himself: "The Son of Man came eating and drinking, and they say 'Here is a glutton and a drunkard...' " "The Son of Man came not to be served but to serve, and to give his life as a ransom for many" (Matthew 11:19 and Mark 10:45).

The first stage begins with the truth that God never makes us His slaves. The purpose of the Gospel is to restore us to the relationship of sons and daughters to a loving Father. "But when the time had fully come, God sent his Son, born of a woman, born under the law, that we might receive the full rights of sons. Because you are sons, God sent the Spirit of his Son into our hearts, the Spirit who calls out, 'Abba, Father.' So you are no longer a slave, but a son; and since you are a son, God has made you also an heir" (Galatians 4:4-7).

The next step in the process is to get back into the slave modality without losing the son-daughter modality. I call this the Slave II Modality. Again our model is Jesus, "...who, though he was in the form of God...emptied himself, taking the form of a servant (slave)" (Philippians 2:6-7). For Paul, likewise, the title, "servant (slave) of Jesus Christ," signified a glorious identity and gave him great joy.

This identity, however, seems to be a blessing that God does not give. Apparently, we have to do it ourselves. The Bible does not say that God makes us slaves. He makes us "sons and daughters" (John), "heirs" (Romans and Galatians), "rulers," "kings," and "priests" (Ephesians, I Peter, Revelation). But Paul says, "I have made myself a slave" (I Corinthians 9:19). If we would have this blessed identity, we must give the gift of ourselves freely to God (Romans 12:1). I think this point is extremely important. If we are slaves to God unwillingly, because we feel this is God's demand—something He has imposed or exacted—there will never be joy in our lives. There will only be complaining (maybe repressed), resentment, and bitterness. Willing slavery, however, brings joy and peace.

It took me some years to realize that this was the root of a spirit of complaining and resentment in myself that I could not seem to get rid of. The signs were disturbingly similar to some of the symptoms of burnout. I noticed in myself a kind of cynical dwelling on ways in which I thought my mission had treated my family and me poorly over the years. This grumbling spirit was clearly wrong, because I knew that God had blessed us and more than "taken care" of our every need through all those years. It kept coming back, though. Each time I thought I had dealt with it and finished it, but after a time, it would pop out and surprise me again. The beginning of a breakthrough for me came when I identified it as the sin of covetousness. A much bigger breakthrough came, however, when I saw the tremendous freedom that could be mine in choosing to be a servant of Jesus Christ—a son of God who chooses joyfully to be a slave....

What is important for us missionaries is that in being both a child of God and a slave of God we are identifying with Jesus. We are free "to be abased, and ... to abound" (Philippians 4:12). We can enjoy without guilt, and we can serve without driven-ness or compulsion, and without a need for achievement or recognition.

Identifying with Jesus, in both His position as son and servant, we receive infinite renewal, healing, and strength.[20]

---

[20]Friest, W. (Apr. 1992)

Summary

It is becoming apparent to those of us in clinical psychology or psychiatry that depression and burnout are illnesses that can affect Christians as well as non-Christians. This book is an attempt to give missionaries and field leaders the tools with which to detect these problems in colleagues and their children. Depression is a treatable illness and treatment may lead to a return to full productive ministry on the field.

Bibliography

Cornwell, P. (1983). *A Time for Remembering*, Harper & Row, NY, pp. 23-24.

DSMIIR, (1987). American Psychiatric Assn., Washington, D.C., pp. 222-224.

Danielson, E. (1982). *MK*, out of print.

Duckworth, J. (Schubert, E.) (1993, in press). The Use of the MMPI and the MMPI II for Selection and Crisis Intervention in Overseas Personnel, *MMPI and the MMPI II, Interpretation Manual for Counselors and Clinicians*, 4th Edition, Accelerated Development, Muncie, IN.

Foyle, M. (1987). *Overcoming Missionary Stress,* EMIS, Wheaton, IL.

Foyle, M. (Jan. 1987). Conference on Missionary Kids, Quito, and personal communication.

Friest, W. (Apr. 1992). The Understanding and Prevention of Missionary Burnout, *Taiwan Mission, Vol. 1, #4*, pp. 4-10.

Gish, D. (1983). Sources of Missionary Stress. *Journal of Psychology & Theology, Vol. II, #3,* pp. 236-242.

Kessler, J., Campbell, R., (1984). *Parents & Teenagers,* Youth for Christ, pp. 201-202.

Maris, R. (1981). *Pathways to Suicide,* John Hopkins, University Press, Baltimore, MD.

Nuss, W. Zubenko, G. (1992). Widows and Depression, *American Journal of Psychiatry, Vol. 149, #3,* pp. 346-351.

O'Donnell, K., O'Donnell, M. (1988). *Helping Missionaries Grow,* Carey, Pasadena, CA.

O'Donnell, K. (Schubert, E.) (1992) Current Issues in Screening & Selection, *Missionary Care: Counting the Cost for World Evangelization,* 1992, Carey, Pasadena, CA.

Oswald, Roy M. (1982). Clergy Burnout: A Survival Kit for Church Professionals, *Ministers Life* Resources.

Pollock, D. (1987). Personal Communications.

Powell, J. (1987). Conference on Missionary Bruising, Detroit, MI.

Schubert, E. (1991). Personality Disorders and the Selection Process for Overseas Missionaries, *International Bulletin of Missionary Research, Vol. 15, #1,* New Haven, CT, pp. 33-36.

Schubert, E. (1993 in press). Personality Disorders and Overseas Missions: Guidelines for the Mental Health Care Professional. *Journal of Psychology & Theology, Vol. 21, #1,* Rosemead School of Psychology, LaMirada, CA.

Schubert, E. (1989). "Bruising in Missionaries." Talk Given at Taiwan Missionary Fellowship, Taichung, Taiwan.

Sehnert, Keith W. (1981). *Stress/Unstress,* Minneapolis, Augsburg.

Seligman, M., (October, 1988). Baby Boomer Blues, *Psychology Today*, pp. 50-54.

Tubesing, Nancy L., and Tubesing, Donald A.. (1984). *Structured Exercises in Stress Management*, Volume 2, Duluth, Whole Person Press.

Vandenberg, Tobia (October 8, 1985). The Invisible Internationals, *The Mennonite*, pp. 484-485.